Moppet on the Run

Story by Jenny Giles

Illustrations by Xiangyi Mo

and Jingwen Wang

"Come and see Moppet," said Laura
to her friend Sally.
"I'm just going to feed her."

The girls walked over
to see the little guinea pig.

"Where is she?" asked Sally,
as they both looked inside the cage.

2

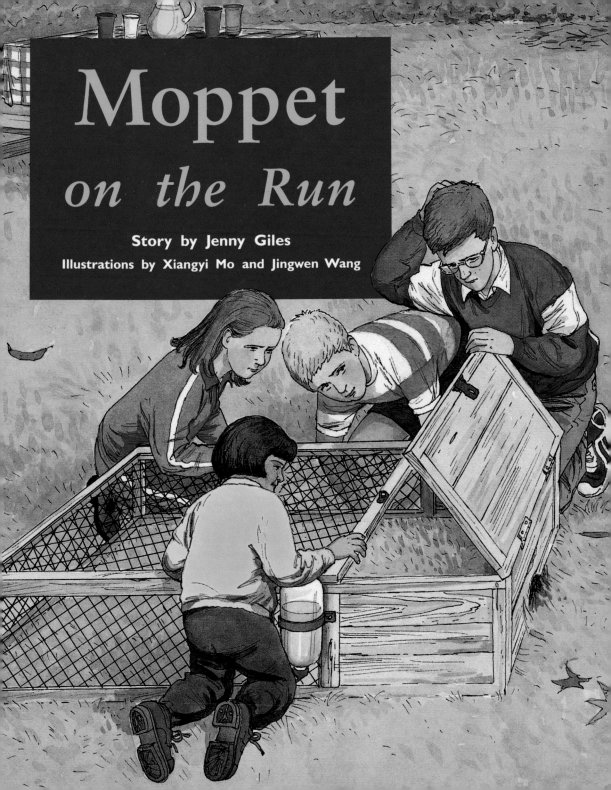

Moppet
on the Run

Story by Jenny Giles

Illustrations by Xiangyi Mo and Jingwen Wang

"Oh, no!" cried Laura. "She's **gone**!"

Sally looked around.
"We'll have to find her quickly,"
she said.
"Dogs get guinea pigs sometimes."

Robert and Harry ran over
to the cage.

"How did Moppet get out?" asked Robert.

"Look!" said Harry.
"There's a little hollow down there
in the grass. She must have pushed
her way out under the cage."

"I didn't think guinea pigs
could do that!" said Robert.

The children hunted all around
the garden for Moppet.

Suddenly, Moppet darted out
from behind a tree.

"There she is!" shouted Laura.
"She's going into those pink flowers."

Harry ran over to the pink flowers
and reached in to get Moppet.

But the little guinea pig
was too quick for him.
She slipped through his hands
and scurried across the grass.

Then she ran into some leaves
and hid there.

The children looked down at the leaves.

Sally said,
"Guinea pigs are hard to catch.
One of ours escaped one day."

"What happened to it?" asked Harry.

"That doesn't matter now," said Robert,
looking at Laura's face.
"Come on! We've got to catch Moppet."

"But how can we do it?" asked Sally.

Then Laura said, "Wait here
and keep watching the leaves.
I've got an idea!"

9

Laura ran over to the table
and pulled the cloth off it.
She raced back to the leaves
and spread the tablecloth over them,
right where Moppet was hiding.
"Hold on to a corner, everyone,"
she said, "and keep the sides down."

The children could see
where Moppet was.
They watched the little bump
she made as she ran around
under the tablecloth.

Then, very slowly, Laura reached out
and caught Moppet
through the tablecloth.
"I've **got** her!" she said.
"But she's very scared.
I can feel her shaking."

Moppet wriggled and struggled,
but Laura held on.
"Quick!" she said to the others.
"Turn the tablecloth over
while I keep holding her."

14

The children smiled as they looked
down at Moppet,
who was trying to run around
in the middle of the tablecloth.

"She'd better stay in there," said Robert,
"while I fix her cage."

"What a lucky little Moppet you are,"
laughed Harry, "going for a ride
in a tablecloth."

"Yes!" said Sally.
"Moppet is **very** lucky...

because Laura thought
of the perfect way
to catch a guinea pig!"

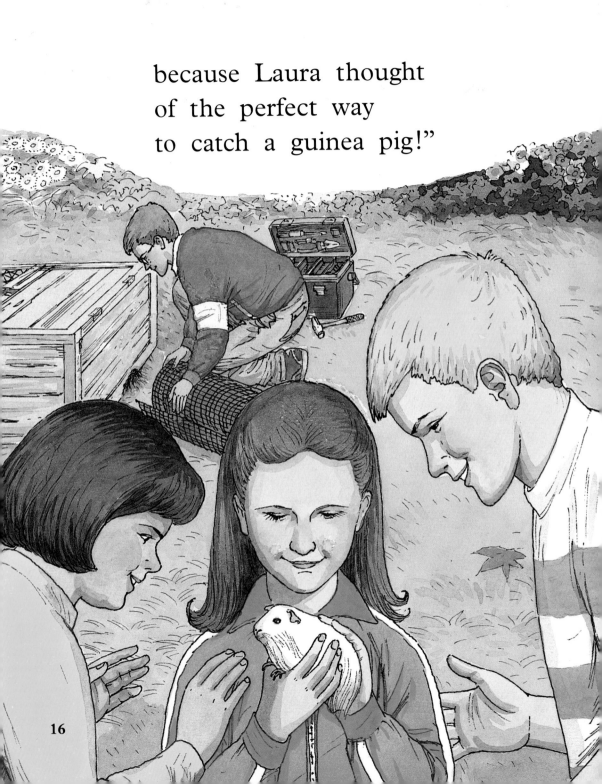